Day of the Speckled Trout

Library of Congress Cataloging-in-Publication Data
Jodon, Mark, 1960-
Day of the Speckled Trout: poems/ Mark Jodon

Library of Congress Control Number: 2015948145

ISBN-13: 978-0692499825
ISBN-10: 0692499822

Transcendent Zero Press
16429 El Camino Real #7
Houston, Texas 77062

Day of the Speckled Trout

Poems by
Mark Jodon

For Kris

When I am
with you

I am where
water

turns
to wine.

Acknowledgments

Mark Jodon is grateful to the following publishers and magazines for giving a home to many of these poems: Bayou River, Sulphur River, Hudson Valley Echoes, Seventh Day Review, Black Buzzard Review, Acorn Whistle, Third Wednesday, Houston Poetry Fest Anthologies, and Austin International Poetry Festival Di-verse-City Anthology.

Several of the poems appeared in *"What the Raven Wants,"* a chapbook published by Provision Press, Houston, Texas.

A special thanks to Dustin Pickering and Z.M. Wise at Transcendent Zero Press.

Contents

PART ONE

PART TWO

PART THREE

Part One

Day of the Speckled Trout

On the day
of the speckled trout
the day each spring
when the fish
leave their streams
and swim through the streets
of our small town
among traffic
beside curbs
and across sidewalks
in the long
cool
shade
of storefronts

These fish swim
to the homes
of our grandfathers
luring them away
from their vegetable gardens
back porch swings and
the women they love
and each year
on this one glorious day
when our grandfathers
rummage through their basements
for fly rods and tackle boxes
we hear again
the soft spoken promise
of mountain streams

**Disposing Extracted Colors
From Ansel Adams' Photos**

The reds he dumped like loose change
in the drawer of his bedside table.

The blues were used as hair rinse
by his great aunt's beautician.

The yellows he pressed like dried daisies
between the pages of the family Bible.

The golds and silvers he sprinkled like confetti
in the folds of letters mailed to his friends

and others he donated anonymously
to churches for stained glass windows.

One time he sprinkled a bit in the batter
of his wife's holiday fruitcake.

Occasionally he slipped some into conversation,
making the words more colorful so to speak,

and the rest he ground with fresh coffee beans
from the A&P for a special morning blend.

Remembering Gravel

Early summer. Thirty years ago.
Piles of gravel rising like mountains
from the city dump's floor.
Mounds of gravel covered in white dust,
dust of dried moonlight,
dust of children's dreams.
Kingdoms of gravel.
Children staking claims to gravel thrones.
Children climbing, their feet slipping, weight shifting, sinking
ankle deep into gravel. Children throwing children
into the window of evening
until their appetites rise above the gravel dust.
Gravel carried home in children's pockets,
shoes and socks to the dinner table.
The taste of gravel on children's tongues.
Gravel dust in the valleys of their hands.
Gravel washed away in the cool shower stream
shortly before children settle down
like dust to dream another day of gravel.

July 4
Monongahela, Pennsylvania

Anticipation follows
the faint whistled rush
across a starless sky.
Children clench their mothers' arms.
They swallow excitement
in one deep breath and
look to the heavens for a sign.
A white iced brilliance
punctures night's membrane.
A firecracker flash
and the heavens spill
emeralds, rubies, and sapphires.
Assembled thunder explodes
like drumfire in the veins
of the hills our grandfathers mined.

Fishing with Pennies

We fish the mouth of Pigeon Creek
where its muddy waters
empty into the Monongahela.
Channel cats feed just beyond our casts
and we are certain
they would take our bait
if only we had longer rods.

Through the valley
a faint breathless breeze
and the whistle of an oncoming train.
We drop our poles and scramble
up the bank on all fours through
thistle and brush across gravel
that skirts the oiled rails.

We lay our heads on the track
while the train is out of sight
and prophesy its coming--
sounds like two, maybe three engines,
coal cars strung end upon end
like circus elephants and box cars
the colors of Christmas.

We lay pennies on the track
a few singles, a couple edge upon edge,
some piggy-backed. Then we slip
into the bush, crouch down and wait,
wondering if something so small
as a dime worth of pennies
could derail the train.

Then, before calm comes
to the track-side greens
we collect what is left of our pennies.
Some are carried away
to Pittsburgh, the Great Lakes, points beyond.
But those that remain
are like no others.

Pennies linked like Olympic rings
thin copper ovals
with wheat-lined borders
an image of Lincoln facing himself.
We pocket our coins
and head for the bank
content with our catch of the day.

Mondrian Flood

Pools of primary color
red, yellow, and blue
separated by thin black
retaining walls for years
withstand the weight
of the visitor's gaze.

Unknown that with each viewing
a microscopic fleck or chip from the walls
falls silently upon the polished
hardwood floors. Until one day
the walls give way to the colors
from drip to drizzle to gush
until the museum is flooded.

Children splash and stomp
in the brilliant colors
chirping like birds with a cat
at the base of the tree.
And the poor gallery guards
in their gray slacks, navy blue blazers
and black leather shoes
trained in museum silence
and hands-off manners
aghast and helpless
not knowing what to do.

Two Holes

On the banks of Pigeon Creek,
part of his childhood deposited
in the dirt and weeds,
a man returns to the spot
where twenty years ago he found
an abandoned fishing boat
hole in its bottom
and he and two friends put to float
taking turns fishing and bailing
with an old mason jar.

He sits with his trouser cuffs rolled up twice,
socks stuffed in the mouths of his shoes
exposing his pale moon white ankles.
He slips his feet into the creek
current running to the Monongahela River
more swiftly than he remembered.
Cold waters born of snow.
He sits till darkness swallows him
waiting to be rescued from the weeds
and the hole in the bottom of his soul.

Lightning

My grandfather lived on Dull Street
in Fair Hope, Pennsylvania –
really he did.
Summer evenings, Pirates on the hand-held,
9-volt transistor radio with Bob Prince
calling the play-by-play,
we sat on the back porch
he in his rocker and I on the glider
hoping for two out lightning late at night,
not a cloud in the sky.

Firemen's Carnival

My father rode the pumper truck
in the Bentleyville Firemen's parade.
Afterwards we went to the carnival
where strings of bare light bulbs
lit wooden game booths above the smell
of cotton candy, caramel apples and
Italian sausage. Outside a steel-barred cage,
a carnival barker dared the bravest
drunken men of this coal mining town
to wrestle a muzzled black bear
sixty seconds for prize money.
We watched four or five men take their turns
climbing into the cage only to be tossed around
like rag dolls to the ground. Men who paid
an hour's wage to entertain us for free.

Waiting for Deer to Feed

Thickening dark woods,
trees like anchors pull night
down to frozen earth.

Half moon
wrapped in blue haze
spills milk light in the clearing

where apples, chopped in half
strewn across blades of black grass,
shine like constellations

and await discovery by astronomers
who each night herd and sweep
this black heaven for fallen stars.

The Surprise

They came from Long Branch and Fair Hope,
from Monroeville and Monessen,
from Turkey Hollow and further down the Mon Valley.
Some came from as far as Martinsburg, West Virginia.

They loaded the trunks of their cars
with potato salad and green bean casseroles,
with fresh baked buns still warm from the oven
for sliced baked ham and hot turkey sandwiches.
There was a pot of stuffed cabbage rolls
almost too heavy to carry,
countless varieties of homemade cookies,
a chocolate sheet cake and a coconut cream pie.

They filled their cars with children and conversation,
talk of seeing brothers and sisters,
favorite stories of aunts and uncles,
and backseat talk of playing with cousins
and climbing the snowball tree.

They arrived at the designated time
at the designated spot
in the alley alongside the edge of the yard,
out of view of the house.
They gathered on the back porch
under the tin awning with scalloped edges,
an area too small to hold this much excitement.
They gave the storm door three brisk raps
and waited silently for an answer.

Through the window they saw his shadow
slip into the kitchen's dark linoleum lake
and then he appeared shuffling toward the door,
moving as fast as his eighty years would allow.

13

They waited for him to unlatch the chain
and open the door before erupting
in a thunderous roar of "Surprise!"

As quickly as this thunder sounded
there was a shower of tears
as this gentle man stood before his family
weeping
because he knew he did not have enough food
in his pantry to feed them.

At the Restaurant

Across the dinner table, a freckled boy,
raggedy red bangs barely above his eyes,
lifts an empty root beer bottle to his lips
blows across the mouth as if to send
an urgent message to his toys: *Hurry! Rescue me!*

I catch his suspecting eyes with an unsolicited story
about Joe O'Delli's corner store where the smell
of freshly roasted peanuts in the summer night
curled through the air like a finger coaxing you
to come near, come in, enjoy;
where the candy counter just inside the door
rose like stadium bleachers, row after row of penny
candy, light and dark chocolate bars, pink bubble gum
cigars five cents a piece.

At the far end of the store, a double glass door
refrigerator chilling bottles of chocolate pop,
an opener dangling on a string
next to the mouth of a metal chute
running down the side of the cooler
through a rough cut hole
in the linoleum floor to a cavernous basement.
Fifteen cents for the drink included the chance to drop
the emptied bottle down the chute and
press an ear over the mouth of darkness
to hear the fainting whisper of the bottle rattle away
and finally crash and shatter onto the concrete floor.

And just as I finish my story, the freckled boy
with the raggedy red bangs barely above his eyes
smiles a mischievous grin brighter than sunlight on
water as he sets free the empty bottle
over the table's edge.

Homer

Each night he spreads the Daily Herald on the library table.
Reads each column with autistic speed. Strokes his beard
and speaks
to no one except himself.
When finished, he returns the paper to the rack,
descends the dog-legged stairs to the ground floor
where Mrs. Byers, perched on her stool
 behind the front desk, glances over
her half moon glasses and mouths the words
"Good night Homer" which he acknowledges
with a monk-like nod as he opens
the screen door and enters the night.
From behind the box-elders he retrieves his old red and
black Schwinn phantom with thick bald tires,
wire basket, red reflectors.
He mounts the torn leather seat
pedals down Main Street passing Chess
Park where the old Italian men
sit on benches talking loudly
with their hands.

Monessen

In this steel town
no need to ask how things are going
if the night sky glows orange.
Steel ingots and slag cars cooling
on the oiled rails above the river.
White and black genies rising
from the mill stacks grant
everyone's wish.

My dad's father lived high above the river
near the water tower. Summer evenings
my brother and I sat on the porch above the garage
in lawn chairs-
the ones with aluminum frames and
green and yellow nylon striped webbing-
watching the drive-in movie screen
miles away on the other side of the river.

From where we sat
the screen was no bigger
than a postage stamp,
gray hues dancing on the hillside.
We made-up the story line
describing in living color
scenes we were too young to watch.

The River Dream

Pigeon Creek rises
beyond its banks.
Dreaming the river dream,
it becomes the river,
swells and swallows
the bridge into town.

A husband and wife
drive home at 2:00 a.m.,
the sweet taste of stories
still fresh on their tongues
after a night of cards
with old high school friends.

They follow the road
to the edge of the dream.
The husband leaves his wife,
walks to the water
and stops where the creek
laps at his feet.

At the point he stops
his father steps forward
and walks waist deep
into the muddy waters.
Halfway out he turns to the bank
and signals his son to follow.

Water, swift and rising,
fills the husband's shoes
as the son's barge-like shadow
ripples on the moonlit path
and holds fast
against the current.

The Water Poets

They hear their names in the rain
splashing on tin awnings.
They don't mind getting wet.

They own no umbrellas, rain slickers or galoshes.
They have birdbaths in their backyards,
plastic rain gauges in their flowerbeds.

They know where every public fountain flows.
Late at night they are silhouettes
in the mist.

They enter dark cathedrals,
secretly dipping their pens in holy water
before writing of sacred, moist places.

New Eagle Hill

New Eagle Hill fills with widows,
women who married men with dark dreams.

Men who left school early to mine the hills
that fed the mills twenty miles downstream.

Men who filled barges one black lump at a time.
Coal dust, buried deep in the mines of their

chests, forming one shovel full at a time
the Hope diamond of death.

Self Portrait

On a canvas of closed eyes
the greens of rolling pasture
bend beneath granite sky
and the fox runs wide-eyed
though no longer hearing
the hound's cry.

McGregor Hill

In the land where
hills have names
the mines beneath
McGregor Hill
burned out of control
for thirteen years.

Weeds withered,
dried and shriveled.
Vines of smoke
climbed out of their roots.

One day the neighbor's dog
caught wind of rabbit,
chased it through the yard
across the gravel alley
down over the hill

and just as it made a quick cut
closing in on the hare
the earth surrendered and the dog
yelped swallowed whole
in a puff of billowing black smoke.

After Fine Arts

First snow. Silent procession
into the night. I didn't hear

You rise from the bed. Snow falling
fine as salt on dark winter greens.

You stand at the window wrapped in a sheet
of moonlight. Frosted glass pane

Hangs like a crystal canvas,
marvelous etching of ice and snow.

Pressing a finger against its cold
you wake me with your laughter,

recalling the gallery guard who
hours earlier kept you from touching the Van Gogh.

Tenancy in Common

Double dutch girls singing
my mother and your mother
hanging out clothes tenancy.

Every time it rains
the rusted tin roof sings
me to sleep tenancy.

Sitting on the front porch
shooting the breeze on a still
summer night tenancy.

Shuffling dominoes and swapping stories
beer bottles sweating rings on
the card table tenancy.

Front door back door wide open
AC tenancy. Hurry close the doors
too many damn mosquitoes tenancy.

Something smells really good
on the stove tenancy. Always room
for another chair at the kitchen table tenancy.

Too young and having too
much fun to know
you're poor tenancy.

Old enough to know now
what this house offered
was never poor tenancy.

Shotgun house a chambered heart
pulsing and beating and embracing
life to the fullest tenancy.

Wherever I am this house I was born in
raised in where I'm going to die in
I take everywhere with me tenancy.

Country

The smell of manure spread thick over tilled brown earth.

A flag of dust flying behind a pickup truck
rolling along the farm to market road.

Its bed filled with wooden bushel
baskets of sweet white corn

dressed in green tasseled dinner jackets.

Menagerie

Out past Walter's Lake
where the road slingshots left and right
an old stone farmhouse sits
without pasture or silo.

Chicken wire cages advertise rabbits for sale.
Hens, like handfuls of feed, scatter
across the front yard in and out
of the junked pickup truck's shadow.

Barefoot children skip through the mouth
of a screenless door into bright
sunlight flashing toothless smiles
their waving palms offered freely
to every passing car.

Robinson Hill

The vacant lot next to the Robinson estate
sloped like a shoulder to an elbow connecting
Fourth Street with Sheridan Alley.

The steep and rocky descent was too dangerous
for our candle waxed Red Flyer sleds.
We waited for ankle deep snow
to use the aluminum saucer sleds we
created by *accidentally* snapping off the handle
on the garbage can lid.

Whoever had the last run of the day
would plunge down the hill shoot across the gravel alley
negotiate the gap in the hedge
and ride the sled to the back porch
of the junior high school English teacher's home
ring her doorbell and try to get out of view without being seen.
We usually learned how successful we were
the next time we had class.

Fireside at my Uncle's Home over Christmas

Strings of red and green lights
splash cheer on the textured ceiling.
Logs crackle, stir and drop
through the hearth's iron hand.

On the cool brick ledge beyond the fire's dance,
a black and white photograph
bears my uncle's handwriting -
Pusan, Korea August 1950.

I turn over the photograph wondering
what my uncle looked like at eighteen
in dress greens, crew cut and boyish smile
and then I see this man in fatigues

next to a mound of bodies
piled like firewood waiting to be burned,
bodies piled like dirt waiting to be bulldozed
into a common grave.

Winter Poem

I open the door
and the tree
of black leaves
becomes barren
once more.

Variation on the Virgin Birth

Christmas Eve, 1971.
The promise of snow
broken by freezing rain.

An acolyte, robed and ready
for service, slips through the crease
of light of the opened door.

He steps into the night
onto rain glazed bricks
slick as a salesman's tongue.

He walks heel toe down the alley
on shards of red and green
traffic light changing beneath his feet.

Each step a separate prayer
for safe passage
until he finally reaches

the spot-lit crèche
delivering the ceramic baby Jesus
to the straw-lined manger.

Black Ants

Faithful friends!
Gather the crumbs
of disappointment
from beneath my table
and store them safely
so that we may have
something good to eat
throughout the long
gray winter before us.

Driving Winter

This is the joy of returning.
The joy of seeing the roadside stand
where sweet white corn sold twelve for a dollar.

The joy of having no appointments
to prevent me from stopping the car
on the gravel shoulder and walking the dirt road

down past the Hermann farmhouse
to the silence of harvest field.
The joy of standing among the remains

of husk and stalk, hearing the crow
in flight against the prison gray sky
cry out "Abba, father."

Part Two

Pine Cove

I sit at the water's edge,
a blanket of dried pine needles
beneath me. An old stump,
bark stripped, weathered, gray
with holes the woodpeckers made,
my quiet companion.

A double-winged dragonfly hovers
over my shoulder, buzzes my ear,
startles me, returns to the water reeds.
Just out of reach from the lake's muddy shore

A pine branch, freed from its trunk
by a recent storm, forks inches above
the calm surface. Balanced at the branch's end
smaller than a fishing bobber, the dark shell
of a young box turtle bathing in sun.

Rising slowly, carefully, I lean forward
for a closer look at the marvelous,
exquisite form that cannot hide
what it was created to become.

Today I Celebrate

The wild blue Texas grass
rising from the roadside ditch.

Three strand barbed wire fence
serving the ranch in silence.

The straight backs of spotted cows
head down in spring.

And the green tractor at rest
in the open field.

Zen Garden

In my garden
there are many beautiful things
I do not know.

Tonight, great joy
to know the yellow blossoms
making their home

in the chicken wire
on the garden wall
are jasmine blooms.

Front Porch, Antlers Inn

Honeysuckle drapes over
a white painted banister.

Champagne fluted petals,
grapefruit red, open into starburst

unveiling the virgin sweet softness
only the hummingbird knows.

Within Sight of Antlers Inn

All afternoon
I sat among
outcroppings
of granite.
The conversation
one-sided.
I said nothing.

Washroom, Antlers Inn

A card post-marked
Llano, Aug. 3, 1909
hangs on the washroom wall.

A Ben Franklin one cent
stamp guaranteed delivery
more than 100 years ago to

Miss Emma Bratton
of Pottsville, Texas.
Miss Lucille queries:

What's the matter
that you quit writing?
I miss your letters.

The Neighbor's Pasture

Fence posts
outline
the neighbor's pasture.

Standing free
of split rail
and barbed wire.

Neither containing
nor excluding
nor possessing.

In late March,
the field hosts
a quiet inauguration

of wild blue grass,
blazing stars and
Indian paintbrush.

Wind off the devil's
backbone
joins the celebration

at the trunk
of a century old
live oak

invisible children
take turns getting
gently pushed on the swing
chained to the tree.

Fence Making

We hand-tie the barbs
of anger on the steel

strands around our homes
twisting them tightly

with pointer and thumb
until our fingers bleed.

We strangely admire our handiwork
unable to understand or explain

our loneliness.

Mojo

Behind the pine curtain
where East Texas swamps steam
and pitcher plants grow wild
devouring unsuspecting prey
there you will likely find it.

Mojo is the man in a red clay field along Route 69
standing arms extended, back arched,
head cocked, chin up, suspended
on an invisible cross against the faint blue Texas sky.

Mojo is the stray dog stopped mid-road in Rusk.
Its penetrating stare piercing your eyes
and haunting your soul. "Ghost dog" people say
the return of a dead loved one come back
to watch over someone in great need.

But mojo runs from the woman in the rainbow striped
cotton housedress in Crockett, her head tightly wrapped
in a flowered
handkerchief, waving garlic stalks and chanting
incantations,
her accent thick as pine sap, you can't understand.

She lives in a white clapboard house
that pulsates in late afternoon sun and
the tree in her front yard decorated
with brightly colored glass bottles dangling from
branches that bare no leaves lure and trap bad mojo.

Bent Man

East Texas pines throw jagged knife
shadows on red clay roads.

Colored bottles dangle from branches
to capture evil spirits.

Every morning on the outskirts of town
a man stands ankle deep in clover

bent over at the waist, arms swinging
like pie tins tied to the cross arms

of a scarecrow. Somehow he knows
when morning sun crowns the pines

and the first ray of light rests upon his back,
it's time for the spirit shadows to release him.

The Scarecrow's Cross

In the harvest field, sitting among
cornstalk stubble, a man spends hours
listening to the wind's sharp tongue.

By dusk, every leaf in the trees surrounding
the field turns against him
siding with the blackbird who all summer

ate in the shadow of the scarecrow's cross
paying no mind to the aluminum
pie pan face chattering in the wind.

Van Gogh Fields

In Van Gogh fields
the rolled bales of hay
reflect on how they
danced in the wind.

The stubble reminds our soles
how difficult it is
to walk in beauty.

Years ago the trees
took sides far enough apart
that neither root nor shadow
ever joined.

Between them a great dance floor
Where the wind tangoed
With golden girls
Night and day.

Can we really say
times were better before
the harvest?

Part Three

First Wind

Sometimes late at night
when the shapes of day
have no form and sleep
has wrestled its way free
from my tired grip,

I go to your bedside
in the squall of silence
that rushes upon me
like a storm that suddenly overtakes
a boat on a lake.

I kneel down beside your bed
and press my head deeper
into the darkness,
closer to the cool bay
of your pillow

and I listen quietly
for the first wind
that swept over the face
of the waters
in each of your tiny breaths.

Pompeii

This morning I listened
as you talked in your sleep.
I could barely hear the words
carried across the crevice
between our two pillows.

You spoke the lost language
of an ancient civilization.
Soft distant words, breathless
warnings of tired messengers
coming too late to save Pompeii.

As sunlight climbed through
our window and fell upon the bed
you turned your back to me.
Your soft distant words fell silent
buried beneath centuries of sleep.

White Canvas

The brush of words
between two lovers spoken tenderly
on the soft pillow of darkness
fills the tiny white canvas
of children's ears awake
in the room across the hall.

Planting Trees

My four year old son
tells me we must plant
these two seedlings
because it is "Harbor" Day.

He tells me
he doesn't remember
the names of these trees
but he thinks

one is Bill, the other Ted.

The Loon

I have never seen the loon,
nor heard its cry.

On the lakes of Minnesota
Robert says it's lonely.

I picture a pond without moonlight,
cattail stalks in the marsh.

Black water sloshing,
something dark,

unseen,
moving.

A Reason To Hunt

A young boy in winter
waits at the window
for his father's return.

A quarter moon clears
the treetops and the boy
watches how blue moonlight

sweeps across the snowy field
and stops in the gritted teeth
of a picket fence.

The boy sees a man
in the distance
separate himself from

the dark bodies of trees
and emerge whole
from the shadows of the woods.

In the open field
the man grows larger
with each step

his body returning
to a form the boy
recognizes.

Watching his father closely
the boy sees for the first time
how his father walks with a slight limp
and how he hides it
by dragging what he has killed over his tracks.

Silhouette of a Man

He sits on the edge of the bed
before a window filled
with morning sun.

His hospital gown is open
exposing the curvature of vertebrae
displayed like an exhibit

Not yet extinct. A cigarette balances
between his lips as he strokes
a lighter over and over again.

Maybe it needs fluid or flint
I tell him as I enter the room.
For a moment he is startled.

Then his expression changes
and his face becomes consumed
with the intense concentration

of a man trying to remember
where he placed something
of great importance.

He struggles for the words to tell me
he no longer desires to smoke
but it's all he now knows he can do.

Moving Boundaries

A silent procession of snow
falls through the night
of my father's death.

I greet the next morning
by opening the side porch door.
Wind rushes to embrace me

like a friend bearing good news.
I reach down for the morning paper
and find a crumpled brown bag.

Inside the bag, a baked ham,
moist and warm, the smell of clove
and ginger rising.

And there in the snow
tracks that cross to my porch
and lead down the hill

move the boundaries of kindness
closer
by that many steps.

The Burial

What have we come
to bury?

Surely something more
than this man.

Perhaps it is the piece
of him in each of us

that we have tried for years
without success to lay to rest.

Oh how difficult it is
to bury what lives within us.

Bequest

To my brother
who knows me
least of all
I leave my heart.

Is it what you expected
after all these years?
Let it rest in your hand.
Tell me how does it feel?

If it is hollow, crawl inside.
Explore it like a new continent.
There are no maps,
no directions, no true north.

You may find children
frozen in snow,
graves without flowers,
a cure for an incurable disease.

If it is heavy,
hold it with two hands--
burdens greater than darkness
are not easily carried.

If it is hard,
drive a stake into it.
Grip it like a gavel and
sentence someone to death.

Swing it like a hammer
and build homes for the homeless
or use it as a mallet
to play croquet.

If it is warm,
scrape off the charcoal crust
with a wire brush and save
the scrapings in a spice jar.

And if it is still
capable of loving,
then give it away
to the first tin man you meet.

Coins

How
he
spent
his
life
left
him
without
change.

Escorts

Suzanne's mother said
you never go alone.
She knew who was coming
for her and she told her daughter
before she died.
Suzanne's husband left
without telling her who
was coming for him
but she suspected who it was.

Sometimes

Sometimes they poke through
the veil that separates us.
Sometimes accidentally, but usually not.
Sometimes it's curiosity, perhaps an opportunity
for a closer look at a newborn grandchild,
so the cradle rocks suddenly
though the child is deep asleep.

Sometimes it's for what they longed to hear before the grave --
an apology, a favorite story, a heartfelt confession.
Sometimes it's to tell you
what they never had the courage to say
(and still don't), so they open a book to someone else's words and
gift them to you.

Or sometimes they knock over
your favorite potted plant to remind you
what you did, their way of saying
you haven't been forgiven.
And sometimes it's just to hurry you
on your way, to give you something to look forward to
or offer comfort and hope
to those you will soon leave behind.

Memories

Some are like
little lunches
we skip or

mean to throw away
and others we save
not knowing if

or when
we'll ever
eat again.

Low Tide

When men walk
the beach at sunset
they see and hear

different things. This evening
on West Beach I see
white pockets of waves

empty failures and
embarrassments
on the shore

and I hear the surf
whisper: *Come,*
claim what is yours.

The Gift

Late at night
a man sits quietly
with his wife.
Her intuition tells her
he is there just to be near her
and as it is her way
she tells him
what she knows of this.

And as it is his way
he does not tell her
he is sharing with her
the gift one man
gives another
when they walk for hours
through woods
without speaking.

Psalm of Praise
For Emily Divine

Beneath her blond straw hat
with turned-up brim,
Miss Emily relaxes
in a weathered-gray Adirondack chair
sipping her salt-rimmed margarita on the rocks.

She requests,
in a soft spoken voice,
a poem for her birthday.
So belated I deliver this gift to her
wrapped in white paper.

A psalm of praise
to the One whose hands
one April morning
placed tender kindness
in her heart.

Destinations
For Tom Kennedy

Remember the time we flew
to Atlanta neither of us
knowing where to go
once we arrived?

Remember how we sat
on a concrete bench in light rain
laughing about our predicament?
Eventually we found our way.

Sometimes when friends walk together
they take different paths to the same place.
We know where we're going.
I'll see you there.

Winter Trees

For Judd & Cynthia

I know men the color of winter trees.
And the women they love
are the birds in the branches
that sing in the snow.

What the Raven Wants

How little progress I've made riding a donkey's back.
I have seen a hundred sunsets between its ears
and tonight I sleep again in the foothills of desire.

I dream the jailor goes home drunk, his ring of keys
dangle from the prison cell lock. In the morning
he returns to find me still chained to my desire.

What do the great black birds know that I have not learned?
They have learned patience as they wait on the wind
for their turn to pick clean the bones of their desire.

I want what the raven wants after forty days of rain.
I want to return home with muddy feet. The dove
with its olive branch is not what I desire.

Why must this longing to return be such a struggle?
If you ask the salmon, it will ignore you as it swims
upstream against the current of desire.

Brother, the holy writings say ask and you shall receive.
I say what you ask for may be what you need
but not what you desire.

Night Sea Journey

When the Maker of Reservations
reserves a night sea journey
in your name, you keep the appointment,
knowing the experience
will be at your own expense.

How good to know
not all storms are meant for you.
Sometimes the reservation
bears the reluctant one's name
and your only job is to throw Jonah overboard.

Remember Noah? He welcomed the rain
but he knew it was coming.
Even the animals knew!
How do you think he got them all on the ark?

Oh friend, how easy to walk on water
when the crying sea is the child you love.
You can run a hundred miles
over the waves before realizing
you've stepped out of the boat.

And who among you ever prayed
for rain longing only for the water?
Lightning and thunder are not likely
to give up their children so easily.

Sometimes the answer to your prayer is just
the ability to stand with muddy feet
after the storm; and if you asked for drink
and were given stones, then tap the rock
on which you stand
for water is closer than you know.

Instrument

How many years have I assumed
the wound was filled with darkness?

The darkness surrounded the wound
but did not enter it.

Inside I discovered light and an instrument
I did not know I could play.

Nobody Knows How Long It Took

He crawled here on purpose
into his wound

and stitched it closed
around him.

When his father died
he emerged a winged body,

a butterfly nobody could catch.

Wild Horses

Our words are like wild horses
the barns of our mouths
cannot contain.

We remember the sounds
of hooves running
into meadows of silence

and how our outstretched hands
grabbed for their tails unable
to return them to the darkness

of their stables. We cry out
to the night hoping the stars
whisper in their turned down ears

Come back, please, forgive us.

Old Clothing

How many years
have we carried
the clothes of our past?

Neatly folded shirts
of despair, spit-shined
shoes of shame

Their polished leather uppers
hiding the gaping holes
in our thinly worn soles.

Isn't it time to
discard the clothes
that no longer fit?

Isn't it time to
set down our boxed
burdens and walk away?

Our callused hands
enough to remind us
who we no longer are.

Wind

There is only one
name for the wind
you resist.

For years you have
walked head first
against it

knowing all along you can
only walk so far for so long
before surrendering to

what you always sensed
but refused to admit was true
since there were times when

the curl of the wind formed
the letters of your name
and your heart cried quietly "here I am."

Then one day when you open
your hands turning palms up
and the seed you held so dearly

is carried away by the wind
you are surprised to learn
you can still hold it forever.

What You May Become

When you live surrounded by
concrete, steel and glass,
you take shallow breaths.
What you breath in
you may become.

Somebody once said
you cannot hear God
if there are no trees.

Tonight I look into the dark face
of a new year. Late December
in the Laurel Mountains,
snow at my feet.

Surrounded by the silent witness
of trees, I take in long deep breaths
filling my lungs with scripture.

Buried Treasure

Wooden gate,
cross-planked center,
the pirate's "X."

Wrought iron handle,
the black handshake
for all who enter.

At dusk, the weathered boards
glow heron blue,
sometimes purple iris.

How different they look in
direct sunlight, the absence
of shadow, flat affect of truth.

But who is to say the truth is
always what we see?
Given the choice I choose

What I feel without touch,
I trust what I know
without seeing; and I praise

What I hear whispered
by the Ancient One
buried like treasure deep in my chest.

Labyrinth

Sometimes the path we walk
is the space between the coils
of a curled up snake.
Its rattles tell us this.

Yet there is comfort
or at least some odd consolation
knowing the path is a labyrinth
and not a maze.

Even though the way concentrically
spirals deeper to the center
no guarantee is given we won't get lost
or finish what we started.

So many paschal mysteries wait within.
Two approaching pilgrims, death and resurrection,
greet us by name, and afterwards strangely
we sense we are no longer the same.

Reaching the center, this point of return,
how difficult to leave this place again
knowing with certainty the path back
will not be the same.

And the golden thread
we laid to guide our return
is the hand of the silent lover
we hold as we walk back together.

Confirmation

I say your name aloud
over and over.
How pleasing to hear
your first name rise, crest
and fall into the wave
of your last name.

Have you ever wondered
if God speaks your name?
I'm sure He does. I imagine
He speaks it more softly
and more frequently than I do.
More than your name is pleasing to Him.

Even now there is a chorus
of angels singing your name
because one said it in the presence
of another who repeated it
to another until it spread
in harmony across the heavens.

About the Poet

Mark Jodon has read his poetry many times at the Houston Poetry Fest as a juried poet, as well as a featured poet. He read as a featured poet at the First Friday series hosted by Inprint and the Nokturne reading series. His work has also been recognized by the Austin International Poetry Festival. His poetry was included in a doctoral dissertation, read in contemplative services, and featured in a photography and poetry exhibition. He is widely published and previously had his chapbook, What the Raven Wants, published by Provision Press. Mark lives in Houston, Texas, with his wife, Kris.

Footnotes to an Unwritten Poem

Fn. 1   The epigraph courtesy of Blake's journal
displayed under glass in the British Museum.

Fn. 2   The familiar fragrance rising from
the third line came from your mother's kitchen.

Fn. 3   The architecture of letters in the middle verse I patterned after
a bombed out European skyline, circa 1942.

Fn. 4   The inconsistent descriptions of the father figure were play-
fully designed to confuse and frustrate my Jungian friends.

Fn. 5   And the address repeated throughout the poem belongs to a
famous painter in Brandywine, Pennsylvania.

Made in the USA
Coppell, TX
03 December 2021

67027362R00056